SHASTA

Shasta

BETH THOMPSON
Katherine Fox

Dedication

To everyone who's ever been told they're too much.

If they tell you to stop blooming, it just means you've been planted in the wrong place.

Contents

Author's Notes

Dear Reader,

In the last two years, I found myself constantly inspired by the natural world, and the people within it. Humanity loves to push its bounds and rebel against the natural flows and rhythms of the world, as if we are not one and the same, our fates intractably intertwined with those of all living things.

I am guilty of the greatest sin of all, which is that of seeing, of feeling, and of pondering, often without the courage to act. I am not an orator, I am not a politician — I am not a doer of great deeds. I am, unfortunately, armed only with eyes and words — words which seem to become less and less of value, as screens strip us of the joys that wait just outside our doors and windows.

It is with joy and humble hope that I pass along these poems to you. This batch reads far more like a challenge, a rallying call than my last — it calls for us to move beyond the self — an extension of the internal healing we must do together that I described in *Walking with Light*. These words are a reminder to myself and to you to examine and change (when possible) the world and society around us.

Maybe they'll spark something within you, too. Root. Sprout. Bud. Bloom. I hope at the very least, this collection of words brings joy and beauty to your days.

Happy Growing,
Beth

Content Warning:

This book contains mentions of topics that may be sensitive including mentions of suicide and trauma, particularly in Section I. Additionally, Section V contains a poem which mentions a disturbing headline the author saw in the news regarding gun violence. These sections may be distressing to some readers.

I

Sowing

Light

It only went half dark.

I looked down
I saw it happen
The panicked face
The lights and sirens flashing
Hazy
Dreamlike
Muted.

A nightmare of my own design
I thought
I didn't want to wake
I fought to sleep.
Tried to turn
My veins to gold

I drifted.
Dark.
Empty.
Between.

Until the light emerged.

A lingering sense.
A presence
A knowledge and a peace
That my time
isn't finished.

That I've got work to do.

Awakening
to tearful sufferers
of my selfishness

But an overwhelming knowledge
an unyielding determination
and a deep understanding

I have work to do
Purpose and light
To spread
And love
To give.

Forgive Me

Forgive me
but forgiving me
Is the hardest thing to do.
(for me)

My body she still
bears the scars
Of days when I almost
Met the stars

And somehow made it through.

Trace the lines I drew in the sand
up and down my arms
I know that you've forgiven me,
Can I forgive myself the harm?

I rest easy now, and always know
The grace that's granted me
Yet every now and then there's nights
when behind my eyes, I see

Ghosts
Of myself when I was gone
Of the girl who lost herself.
I'm still here.

Some days:
No matter who forgives me
I forget how to
Forgive myself.

Fibro

You are too young
To hurt this much.
Bones
that feel lined —
Lined with needles —
with worry —
Prickling.

Muscles
wrapped in cotton
Mind
not your own

Shrouded
Clouded
Heavy
Slow
Forced rest.

Burlap and Silk

Wrap it in silk, caressing and soft
So fine, so perfect, and clean
An intricate pattern, poised and divine
hiding its secrets, unseen

Reinforced with burlap, grating your skin
Blistered, you try to hold on
The world sees the fine, but we felt the truth
Exposure — the fear we lived on

Two generations pass, and somehow it flipped
Now grime has consumed our world
Chaos is the truth and I need to escape
my tired hands stay tightly curled

I cannot afford to pay for both sides
To use the same fabric that's stitched
I stand here with cotton and seek to move on
Setting fire to the burlap and silk

Down 80

Down 80
Driving 79
To a place I thought I found my kind
Down to the wire, decisions we can't make
Down to who we think we should be.

Up to a high
Up on my own lies
Running from quiet and my own mind
Bought into my own time

Illusions are fair in the bright autumn air
When everything new seems a promise or dare
The world unconstrained and you've turned off the pain
your soul is free though they thought it was tamed

You had it all
You set it in flames
Now there's a hole in your past
Like you never were there and nobody will care
At least they were the ones to outlast

Beside the mighty you were so small
you bought your own shit and thought you had it all
You lied to yourself and you lied to them
The people who thought you a capable friend

Failure, Emptiness, Lies, Untruths
The river will flow it away
Along with your memories — Empty and blank
You weren't there and not destined to stay.

Down 80
Down 79
Down to a place I thought I found my kind
Down to the wire and decisions we can't make
Down to who we think we should be

It haunts me sometimes when the air turns crisp
Those days and who I could have been
Tell me why it still lingers, when here in my fingers
Why do I need the past when I'm me?

Time Back

I thought
that my time
was up.

I was ready.

When hell or heaven spits you out

It's hard not to believe
there is a reason

And I will spend
Every
Last
Gasping breath

Proving myself deserving.

When time is a gift you didn't think you'd get
It feels like
you're running
on borrowed moments

How to explain the paradox

Of endless extra time
Feeling like it's slipping through your fingers
Running out of time.
Unworthy of the gift.

Out of Time

The gift
God looked me in the face and said
Not yet
Only one life, not nine — not to waste.

Fueled by fury of the dying
Take advantage of this, I'm trying
Mostly frantic, seeking to fulfill
Most days all you see is overkill

Driving myself straight to madness
trying to outpace this sadness
running from demons that scream out
Killing any final sense of doubt

Boxing out risk of normalcy
yet dying for peace, my chance to be free
Torn against self, I cannot fall
so many times... I've lost it all.

Make it worth creator's effort
Probably could've picked someone better
Grappling the shadows of the clock
Looking down the barrel of time's glock

Gifts are given sans condition
Trying to realize the vision
Need I be worthy or can I breathe?
What is up God's sleeve?

Running

Remember
The adrenaline
Of running
From yourself
From danger
From scars
No home, no love, so far
From self.

My bones recall
The ghost of loneliness
My ache to be cradled
A reminder
My body cries
With remembrance
Each pain
A scrapbook
Of days gone by

The body
She is sharp
She knows
How it goes
She forgets
That she doesn't need
To run
Anymore.

Suck Me Dry

Suck me dry
to purify
head games, light
And heavy sighs

Sometimes when I'm disappearing
is the time I'm really hearing
Tuning fork to Gaia's feeling
Cut before I hit the ceiling

To fight the heaviness of life
I fancied self, a Venus wife
Or Athena's wisdom, sage
Yet Artemis' truth is writ in rage

The voice of earth is pulling down
alight with atoms all around
The slightest push or pull will set
my madness spinning off and yet

To channel light, I train and seek
so never might I have to leash
the inner fires and gifts of mine
To walk with light, in light we shine

Off the Rails

Family train, going down the tracks
Engine running, full of gas
Full on speed from overseas
Suddenly going nowhere fast

Off the rails, something cracked
Spilling coal and oil and gas
Filling lungs with tar and smoke
Against the damage, is there hope?

Engineer throws on a half-assed patch
Leaking pistons, poison gas
Trails are broke, nature poisoned
Still somehow the show must go on

Off the rails, the broken trails
Impact echoes in my bones
How to heal it so more don't feel it
Building this new home?

Outside
warm lights glow,
hazy cover-up show
Inside
the impact's ring
Baby is crying,
mother's heart dying
They've displeased the king

Impacts we still feel, somehow we must heal
Broken trails lead us to home

Off the rails, tooth and nail
Impact rattles your bones
How to heal it so more don't feel it
Building this new home?

Our earth shattered, quaking
Ancestral wisdom is lost
How could they know the shadows would grow, and
We would be bearing the cost

We must heal the damage, we cannot bandage
Or sew up with lies and mistrust
Struggling up mountains, seeking heaven's countenance
Raising ourselves from the dust

Off the rails, the broken trails
Impact echoes in my bones
How to heal it so more don't feel it
Building this new home?

We are the ancestors we seek
Now is not the time to be meek
Heal the wounds of the past
To build our universal family, and last.

It's Okay

It's ok
It's ok
It's ok
To be "okay"

Big dreams, big ego
Name known
It's a big show
I want it all
I have to give
Put on earth to grow and live

Just remember
It's okay
And the best gift
You could ever give
Just to be "okay"

Through hell and back
With scars and cracks
You won't believe what
Lil' old me has seen

The biggest blessing I can have
Isn't fame or titles, cash
No matter what I *think* I need

It's just to rest
To slow it down
To Live and be "okay"

When Hell has called
And you did fall
Were chewed up, burned, clawed back

It's easy to feel the demon's breath
In each goosebump that's down your neck
Although you could slow down

They forgot to tell us
We don't have to run
We don't need to *seek* love

We're surrounded by it everywhere
Breathe it in —
And be "okay"

Feel the sun beat on your skin

Pause, and let the energy in
The universe conspired for you
All you need
Is to be "okay"

Knowing Better

I wasted
A great deal of my life
Believing I knew better

When in fact...

I just saw differently.

II

Rooting

Possibility

The endless possibilities are eating me alive
The thoughts of mediocrity will kill me from inside
Poisoned thoughts of all the wasted days gone by
Paralyzed by knowing Time is one thing you can't buy

Is the path I tread a consequence of being someone else?
Is staying in one place a fatal cancer for my health?
Or is stability the greatest blessing I have found?
A safe and loving haven for dreams too big for myself

They say you die when time forgets the things you say
and do
So I will flail and rail and wail these words until I'm blue
A translation to make you see the world as it can be
A cry unto eternity, this is my gift to you

So many paths that we can tread and ways to leave
our mark
I run and cry and try to thwart each day's impending arc
Forgetting here and now is where the hearts I love
must live
And in each present moment — now — is where we're
called to give

Possibilities and ego could just be the end of me
Driving my restless soul to bring me to insanity
If I die and fade away, is it calamity?
Not as long as I'm immortalized in love to family

Can I measure possibility in love and hearts I knew?
A lasting impact made from kindness treasured, real
and true
Hold me in peace and memory and please do not forget
Even if in history's arc, a place I do not get.

Slinkies

Some folks' lives unwind before them
like a slinky.
Spiraling slowly
down the stairs of their life
resting
between each step yet
brought ever downward
from their goal
by the self-perpetuating backward momentum of each
choice they make

Slinking
through their lives
that are not their own
driven by every wind blowing their way
just trying to get by unnoticed
refusing to stir the pot
to make a noise
to brew something incredible
to notice the burning stench of their own home
unheeding of the signs
directing them towards a life which could be lived -
truly lived —
if only they'd read the signs

And there's nothing *wrong* with that
I'm kinda jealous.

I refuse to sit
to let the timer run out
to not move to give up
to cry Uncle to rest on the laurels of my unfulfilled
dreams
and I refuse to live my life one more minute in the.
company of those
who will pull me back.

push me forward
hold me up in my darkness
and share in the light that is our greatness
Striving, moving
Urging me forward

I choose to *live* my life.
You can join me.
But you have to choose.

Measuring a Life

Your worth is not
measured by productivity
despite what your anxious mind
and capitalist urges
might whisper to you
at night.

Your life's work
is not calculated
in spreadsheets.
Your story won't be told
in an annual report.

Your mother's love
can't be won
by spotless floors, clean cabinets
and a gleaming stove.

Instead:

If you must measure your worth
measure it in joy
in the length of your hugs
the depth of your kisses
the width of your smile

Love unconditionally
Love without hesitation
Love beyond color, borders, and creed

And most of all
Love yourself
Often.
Much.
And endlessly.

Memory

I want to be a god
I want to be remembered
I want to walk large
I want my footprints to stamp their imprint
Into the pages of history
So hard
That the ink drips down
Even after the chapter turns

I try to do no harm
I try to walk with light
I try to live in love
I try to carry myself with quiet dignity
And rest in the arms of my loved ones
So soft
Beloved for my truest self
Held in the hearts of my angels

What do I want?

I just

Don't

want
to be

forgotten.

Birthday

What is a birthday?
On this day in history
Two people created breath

On this day
two in love
made
a miracle.

You came full of life and full of love

The gift —
We can renew it every day.

Each moment fulfilled
is a moment of birth
running over with thanksgiving
triumph over death and dark

Live in the light
Born of earth, fire, sweat, skin
consecrating the gift of love

It is your fate — your destiny
to live
to be love.

Fulfill the prophecy
Be born to it, not only today, but always.
Let every day be a day of birth.

The Journey

Don't hide where you came from
It made you

But.

you're not there anymore.

Don't fear where you're going
It will be
as beautiful
As you make it

Eyes up, warrior.
We fight and thrive in the dark.

III

Sprouting

Brave

Let it go
Your ego and bluffs
Smoking candles, a burnt out snuff
Raise your firsts to curse it all
Drop them low and let it call

Everything that is not love
Is cowardice
Lay yourself
To bare your bliss
Surrender to the one abyss
Plug into your consciousness

Be a brave, find it all
Knocked down, dropout, heed love's call
Ditch the bottle, forgo the small
Rise above the lies, don't fall

Everything that is not love
Is cowardice
Lay yourself
To bare your bliss
Surrender to the one abyss
Plug into your consciousness

New warriors, swordless, all I sing
No country, borders, crowns or kings
Common thread and common breath
Life sans love is truest death

Everything that is not love
Is cowardice
Lay yourself
To bare your bliss
Surrender to the one abyss
Plug into your consciousness

When Hades rears his ugly head
Cling to love and deny the dead
Hold my hand, within a glove
And let it go, stay with love

Another song for peace and love
I guess we'll never have enough
Reading the script yet still at war
children, we've been through this before

Everything that is not love
Is cowardice
Lay yourself
To bare your bliss
Surrender to the one abyss
Plug into your consciousness

Let it go and get it right
Pray love can save the world tonight

Bulletproof

Resilient
Iron Maiden
Steel Magnolia
Lucky

They call me indestructible, or so the gods must believe.

The bulletproof

are the ones who carry
the world on their shoulders

Yet walking within me
Is the young girl
who never got

her wings

Worlds unexplored
because the only choice
was survival

How can I curse the gods
When they made me bulletproof?

I just wish the materials
were a bit more flexible

As I pray
I won't break
not from bullets
but from shattering
against the oncoming storm

The strong must hold fast
and pray that we do not break

So strong
we cannot bend or weave
Even if we wanted to.

The consequences of being bulletproof.

Recognition

Restless wanderer, seeking out peace
Hiding in corners, yearning to be seen
Making friends with shadows, cursing to the ground
Desperately asking where under the sky you've been

Lonely soul, praying for the road
Looking for signs both high and low
Will I find me? Will I rest?
Body, soul empty, somehow I know

Out there you were, waiting for me
Recognition of counterparts in eternity
When I held your hand, when I felt your soul
I discovered true rest, because now we know

With the light of our match, a flickering chance
Held in eternity's unwavering dance
Intertwined and vibrating higher we'll fly
Wholly fulfilled even after we die

Holding on tighter, I was born a fighter
I promise I won't ever let go
Writing our story, lighting up the night sky
Our love is an unending flame

Because out there you'll be, waiting for me
Recognition of counterparts in eternity
When I held your hand, when I felt your soul
I discovered true rest, because we both glow

The emptiness fell when I looked in your eyes
Anguished nights seeking, are now soft sweet sighs
Belief in a thing I had given up seeking
A loner who boasted, is humbled, believing

Hold me forever, our souls fly together
Never forsaking the light that we cast
Unspoken secrets you know that you keep this
Wandering heart safe and calm

At the end of the night you'll be waiting for me
Recognition of counterparts in eternity
If I lose your hand, I'll still find your soul
My self will not rest, I will find your soft glow

When the last night falls, when the steam engine calls
Passengers it's time to go
No matter the trains we board, I know my reward
I will always find you at the end... of the road

Small

Small and powerless
Stinging hot bitterness
Don't believe the lies.

You can fly.

Impermanence

You never know
how much someone mattered
until you realize
all you'll ever have
Is memories.

Appreciate loved ones
while they're here
because death
isn't any easier
Even if you're expecting it.

Mercenary

If you have to say
"I'm one of the good ones"
It may be time to reconsider
your *profession.*

Black and blue aren't the same hue.

Heroes

The best kind of people
are the ones who fall for heroes
for stories
for legends

People who believe
that written in these tales
is the promise of who we could be.
Who we should be.

Who we are.

IV

Budding

Biomimicry

*"Biomimicry is when humans take inspiration in, or engage
in behaviors drawn from, the natural world."*

A postulation:
Biomimicry isn't real
We call it "mimicry" as though we're apart:
we long to separate ourselves
from the animal
the natural within.

Step into it.

become whole

You, I, we — do not *mimic* nature
We *are* nature.

We can re-become it.

Like a re-remembered tune
when you watch the sea
remember what it means
how it feels
to move as one
to flow, to crash, to let go

to dissolve the barriers of otherness
wash yourself away into the great oneness

Feel the sun on your skin
recall warmth
beyond the thermostat
beyond walls
the walls we build between each other and this place
melt away the lies we've told ourselves

Nature is our home
Our mother
Our teacher
Re-remember
Re-become
Transcend back

Transition Time

Everything comes alive in Autumn,

So much begins!
Children at school
Holidays; celebrations; harvest.

The entirety of humanity holding onto Activity.

Even Nature seems brighter
showing off
one more time before rest.

Clad in her finest array of gold
before we all give way
to slumber

Fall

Fall
is destabilizing
My libra soul
is the leaves
falling
Drifting on the wind
not knowing
where we would fall
Only
that
we would

Chaos leaves more scars than you think

Gravity

What goes up must come down
Thank god for Balance

Gravity's inevitability
Its pull — we fight this law

How human of us
to think we are special
and that we know better

Root to the earth! Our mother!
Why the fascination with space
When all we need
is here?

Root me down
To the ground
Free and tethered
Safe

Gravity reminding me
Secure and held we are
To rest.

Spider's Web

The spider springs with father Time
we race against the clock.
Beady eyes, gossamer wings,
frenetic, hastened shocks.

Falling rains can't wash away
our self inflicted pain;
Don't race inevitability —
save yourself the strain.

The handheld glow we've come to know
promises escape from pain
and silent hooded figures board
a Hades, Hell-bound train.

Save yourself by tuning in
to a different frequency
Close your eyes
and realize 4K isn't how we see.

Two different ways to surrender
to Time's incessant flow
Inevitably at the end of the line,
we all become the glow.

Breathe and feel your cells embark
into the universe
Or let yourself be pulled into
regret, the final curse.

One In

One in a million sunflowers lined up to face the sun
In dancing rows of yellow bursts, out of many, one.

One seed dropped in the fields
And tended to with love
Is still entitled to grow and change
with showers from above

Your gifts, abundant, make you
One of a million souls
Deserving of eternity
Still in a *human* mold

Fractal Patchwork

We have become
Fractals
shattered and scattered
at war.

Coalesce.
Converge.
Take lessons from songbirds and soar

beyond our brokenness.
Awaken to your humanness
and fly

Look below at the fractals of color
Weaving together into
A tapestry
From afar
the many are all
just One.

Confluence

Down at the water's edge
where the reeds poke their tips to the sky
and the shadows of the trees kiss the sun-washed banks
I sit at the confluence

I sit at the confluence, where the river splits, or comes
together
A matter of perspective
my soul recognizes the water
fluid, just like me

Tortured and dark
or still and bright
Depending on the weather
Lovely outside
And turbulence within
Two sides that come together

Will I ever find my confluence
in that place where I am whole?
Dark and light they split my skin,
the battle for my soul

I seek wisdom in this place
Longing to know what's real
In this river's winding bends
Are the million things I feel

V

Blooming

Pictures of the Day

"School Girl Shot -"
"United Pakistanis 14-year-old campaigner for education
rights -"

Ironic that she educates us long after her death
callous captions facts avoiding bias —
How can we not be so?
Human rights violated —
just black ink across a page and I see red
the words don't do justice to the horrified
screams of anguish and fear
which must have echoed in the ears of photographers
and

echo in mine

I see it.
Red blood on green water
a christmas of hate and the gift
that they give us is a picture show
watching on the TV set

Yet what do we give our attention?
our pity
Do we truly give our hearts?

Love is action.
if you feel it, do it.

No screen
can move the mountains
No magazine
can change the world

Until
we move
together
our hands outstretched
then the pictures of the day
will continue
to move
in their virtual reality

Courting Favor

Who are you?
Who do you want to be?
How much can you hide away
from all the things you see?

Empty spaces, empty chair
Empty heart, no love left there
Empty handed, beg for scraps
A lonely scar to share

Court their favor, masked saccharine nature
Is who they see who you should be?
How long can you play the role
until the emptiness fills your soul

Replace remains written by gain
bend at the goddess' hall
Hollywood might sound so good
But will it take it all?

Court their favor, masked saccharine nature
Is who they see who you should be?
How long can you play the role
until the emptiness fills your soul

Don't allow me to just be another
spread your wings now and fly my brother
Don't accept paper, don't court their nature
Fill yourself with the truth...
be whole.

Dying to Live

Dying to live
to feel it in full
Holding on tight yet desperate
to ride the wave

Chasing a high to escape
testing how close to death you can fly
the high is *life*

And the rest is a lie.

When you're dying to live
and you're living a lie
You're walking with death —
hope you get out alive.

Given

"We gave you life
And we can take it away"

The aunties angrily titter
At babies
And husbands
And teens

Bitterly remembering
The lives they let slip away — old dreams

That others might have theirs
The only weapons left to them
Are sharp tongues
And pointed glares.

Control

They'll take you empty
As long as they can take you
They'll rob your power
as long as it can become theirs

They're scared.

Scared of how they lost control
Scared they'll never get it back
Scared of the world without boundaries

They're human
they don't know.

Nature's got it under control
she will hold them
if they just let go

Fear rules us all.

Break free — find love.

I Believe

Even cars run on autopilot now.

GPS tells you where to go.
Boss tells you when.
K-12, college grad, 9-5 and then...

burnt out and shut in
eyes glued
Why am I so tired

Do you really wonder?
No energy left except to consume.

To be shaped and molded
too empty to create and fill your cup

I believe
We can move beyond this

I believe
we can remember

How to create
How to think
How to love

Radically re-imagine your life

Remember who you are.

Robot

You don't need
to completely
drain your battery
before plugging
yourself
back in.

You're not a robot
You're soul and skin.

White Lies

Choking on this glitz and glamor,
playing parts to hear them yammer
Pay to play and by the rules,
Russian roulette with master's tools
Rubbing elbows with the liars,
crying heart, throw you a flyer
Paid your ticket,
welcome to the show... but you know...

Pakistan drowning, while we're all crowning
But it's alright
Australia burning, humans not learning, indigenous
cries...
white lies

Desperate to be the solution,
try to change it, but it's clued in
System's broken, time to take it down... turn it 'round.
Slowly burning, take your yearning,
accolades, just turn the page...
Nature's rage... she's uncaged

The show rolls on whether you're playing,
Wasted away our godly praying,
stoke the flames
Sit and watch it burn... while you yearn

Pakistan drowning, while we're all crowning
But it's alright
Australia burning, humans aren't learning, indigenous
cries...
white lies

Talk to the warriors in flooded streets
plagued by heat with no place to sleep
Tell them that it will be all alright... green and white

Bring it in, build coalition, rainbow patchwork
Find the vision... find... stop the lies

Pakistan drowning, while we're all crowning
But it's alright
Australia burning, humans aren't learning, indigenous
  cries...
White lies

Mama lion finds no water, empty savannah, creation's
daughter
Stripped... give your gifts... give your gifts...

Make it real... make it real...

Can we heal?

The Tortured Souls

I'm not mean
I'm not wrong
I'm not dumb
I'm not lying

I don't think
I don't act
I don't look
Like anyone else.

and it's painful
and it's hard
it's like a howl resounding off pale granite walls
echoing into the pit
of nothing
on the deaf ears and hearts of the masses.

It's lonely.
It's tortured souls
It's crying out to one another across the sky
It's hoping that someone is listening.

Just touch me
Just hold me
Just teach me

That I'm not crazy
That I'm not alone
in the end.

Sanguine

You're sanguine, so serene
hid away beneath a sheen

Glittering surfaces, tempered glass
just a way to cover your ass

Look once, check twice
Something old could be twice as nice

Lion's tame, behind glass panes
muted roars, that's why you came

Under wraps, spirits don't soar
I'll share mine if you share yours

Safety locks and soulless rocks
What happens when the system blocks

Spidered cracks, one tiny hole
All it takes to touch a soul
Watch damage bled, or free your head
Glitter spreads, they want you dead

Open wide, don't go inside
Feel the real, don't try to hide

Rough and raw, your honesty
May help others to walk free.
Let it be...
And then we'll see.

Painted

We are
Painted
With masks
Of expectation

Colors
We delicately brush
Inside the lines of
Who
And What
We're supposed to be.

At a certain age
a size
fitting
squeezing inside a box
Or
on a scale
"This is your allocated space"
In a 2-dimensional world

Only stroke
in black and white
don't splash bold colors
Neon, fuchsia, gold, aquamarine
A rainbow
splattered
on the masterpiece
only you can make

Let's rip the canvas off
Let's fling glitter wide
Cast the glint
Of our one bold, precious sun
Glisten
into every corner
of this technicolor world

Dance through gilded streets
clothe yourself in crimson defiance

Let yourself expand
Be big, be bold
Color
every inch and corner
You can reach
become intimate with every hue

And never stop creating
the messy, gorgeous, masterpiece
That is your soul,
your heart,
your mind,
your only precious life.

Lost

8 billion people
I think it's more now
A planet cracking under our weight

What if we walked with light?

Medicate

Take me off the oxygen
Blood pumps heart beats again
Colors brighter than I knew
shine intensely, I just may blow through

Medicate, medicate, medicate me
Medicate the beast so you don't have to see
the mess you made
Aren't you glad you stayed?

Prick your finger, pull the trigger
Pull the plug, the shock delivered hurts.
Momentary integration, pulling back this numb
sensation
see the truth and let the colors glow... now you know

Your light within could crack you open
if you leave your truth unspoken
Crackling energy beneath the skin
If you're ready, it's time to begin,
to fix our sin

Medicate, medicate, medicate me
Medicate the beast so you don't have to see
the mess you made
Aren't you glad you stayed?

Build the world that came from dreamers
All the dark "would-have-been-ers"
Look outside, take your lesson from the trees
Let their wisdom bring you to your knees

The tasks at hand are too demanding
Pull your hair, blood, last ones standing
Too much pain, don't try to plug back in

To save your skin

Medicate, medicate, medicate me
Medicate the beast so you don't have to see
the mess you made
Aren't you glad you stayed?

I used to be so damn numb
Now some days I'm overcome
Broken by my own possibility
I'm set free

Will you open up your story?
Redefine your sense of glory
build the truth, set fire to the machine

Rebuild clean.

About the Author

Beth Thompson lives in the Chicago suburbs with her husband, Jason. In her free time, Beth loves to practice and teach yoga, spend time outdoors gardening, hiking and biking, reading, and volunteering her time to worthy causes.

Though this book explores mental health and some themes of generational trauma, it also explores how we can change the world for the better. If you feel this calling, I guarantee it is a difficult road, but a rewarding one that is more than worth it. It is the sister title to the author's first book, "Walking with Light."

Regarding the above mention of mental health, please see the below hotlines if you are struggling, and remember you are never alone. Sometimes it is the most beautiful souls who struggle the most.

If you or someone you know is having thoughts of suicide or experiencing a mental health or substance use crisis, 988 provides a connection to free, 24/7 confidential support.